SHAPED BY HER HANDS

POTTER MARIA MARTINEZ

ANNA HARBER FREEMAN & BARBARA GONZALES
ILLUSTRATED BY APHELANDRA

ALBERT WHITMAN & COMPANY
CHICAGO, ILLINOIS

MARIA POVIKA grew up surrounded by clay. It was in the earth under her deerskin untōhs, in the thick adobe walls of her pueblo home, and in the large jars that held her water, gathered from the nearby Rio Grande.

While her parents planted the fields and ground corn, young Maria tried to make playful clay bowls. She left them in the hot New Mexico sun to dry, but each one cracked and crumbled.

The Tewa people in San Ildefonso had been making and using pots for centuries, but in the 1890s, many people were buying tinware from factories instead. Little Maria's ko-ōo, Nicolasa, still made strong clay pots, so Maria went to her home in the plaza to ask for help.

Aunt Nicolasa was happy to show Maria the centuries-old tradition of san-away. Together, they gathered clay and thanked Mother Earth for sharing with them.

Nicolasa showed Maria how to mix the clay with water and volcanic ash, and how to roll coils between her hands to build the pot's walls.

As the two of them worked, Nicolasa told Maria about the importance of sharing clay knowledge. She wanted Maria to know how to make pots to store seeds and grains in, so their Tewa traditions would live on.

As Maria watched Nicolasa work the clay, she thought of the many generations of potters who had come before. She wanted to make bowls as strong and beautiful as her ko-ōo's.

While her sisters played with their straw dolls, Maria practiced.
After months of working with the clay, Maria's confident hands
were making sturdy, round bowls. Nicolasa decided to let her fire
her first pot. Firing the pots hardened them and made them strong,
but not every pot survived firing.

On a clear day without a whisper of wind, Maria helped her ko-ōo build the pottery fire. Together, they placed wood and chips of dried cow manure around a stack of pots. She watched Nicolasa light the fire and say a prayer, and they sat down to wait.

Maria and Nicolasa sat for hours in the fire's glow.
Finally, the pots were done. Thinking of her bowls that
crumbled in the sun, Maria held her breath as Nicolasa
used a stick to pull her pot out of the ashes.

It was perfect!

Maria carried the pot home, cradling it like a baby.
Her mother, her yeya, proudly placed it beside the fireplace,
and put cornmeal inside for spiritual blessings.
Maria's heart glowed.

As a teenager, Maria went to boarding school with her sisters, but she missed the clay and life in San Ildefonso, so as soon as she could, she returned to her home in the pueblo.

The twentieth century began, and Maria met a young man named
Julian Martinez. They fell in love.

In their marriage ceremony, they drank water from the spouts
of a wedding vase Ko-ōo Nicolasa had made for them.

Maria and Julian Martinez inherited a house in the pueblo.
Their hands grew busier as they worked and cared for their children,
but Maria never stopped making pots, and her reputation grew.

In 1908, an archaeologist named Edgar Lee Hewett came to see Maria. Mr. Hewett had heard of Maria's skills while working at a nearby dig site. He asked Maria if she could create a pot based on an ancient sherd of black pottery that had been uncovered on the dig.

Maria had never made anything polished as fine, or fired so black.
She knew it would take hard work and patience, but she wanted to try.

Maria and Julian dug clay and began
experimenting. She polished her pots using
a river stone. Then, they tested many ways
of firing the pottery.

One afternoon, they tried smothering the fire to keep the smoke in. When they pulled out the pot, it was shiny, and black as a raven.

Mr. Hewett had hoped only that Maria could recreate the ancient piece of pottery, but what he saw in these pots was something old and new, and entirely unexpected.

They were magnificent.

Mr. Hewett knew others would want to see them too.
He put one of the pots in the Museum of New Mexico,
where he worked, and brought the others to shops in
Santa Fe. They sold right away.

Maria had never sold her work before. She was amazed that people wanted to buy pots shaped by her hands.

Julian began painting intricate patterns, feathers, and water serpents onto Maria's polished pots using a yucca-blade brush.

These black-on-black pots sold as fast as Maria and Julian could make them. Maria needed more hands to keep up with demand, so she taught her friends and relatives to help. Blackware flourished in San Ildefonso.

Over the next two decades, Maria and Julian were invited to demonstrate their pottery making in New York, San Francisco, and Chicago.

At first it felt strange to have others watch her work, but Maria remembered Nicolasa's words about sharing what she knew.

When Julian died in 1943, Maria's heart
and pots felt empty without her husband
and partner. But she had spent her whole life
sharing clay with her family.

First, her children came to paint the designs.

Later, her grandchildren came to help with
the painting and polishing.

They made pots as a family, remembering
to thank Mother Earth, and teaching
new hands to form, polish, and design.

"The Great Spirit gave me [hands] that work...
but not for myself, for all my Tewa people."

MARIA POVIKA MARTINEZ: HER NAME

At birth, Maria was named Povika, meaning "Pond Lily," in her native language of Tewa. *Maria* was added at her christening later in life. As Maria's pots became more famous, a variation on the spelling of her name, *Poveka*, began to be used. This is possibly because some curators and scholars were unfamiliar with Tewa. Others may have mistaken the looped *i* on her signed pots for an *e*, so that her name appeared to be Poveka. Many museums and sources still use this spelling, but her family and this book use the Tewa spelling, *Povika*.

MORE ABOUT MARIA

Maria's exact date of birth is unknown. During her life, Maria's unsurpassed skills with clay elevated Native American Indian pottery to a fine art, and she was awarded several honorary doctorates. Maria was invited to the White House on several occasions, and John D. Rockefeller Jr. even asked her to lay the cornerstone of Rockefeller Center in New York City. Throughout her eighty-year career, Maria remained a strong ambassador for her people. She died in 1980, surrounded by family in San Ildefonso Pueblo.

THE TEWA PEOPLE AND SAN ILDEFONSO PUEBLO

San Ildefonso Pueblo is surrounded by mesas and mountains north of Santa Fe, New Mexico, and is home to about one thousand people. It is one of nineteen Pueblo tribes in New Mexico, and one of six Pueblo tribes in which people speak the Tewa language. Each Pueblo community is a sovereign nation with its own government.

The Tewa people of San Ildefonso have maintained a strong sense of identity and way of life over the years despite facing many challenges, including encroachment on their land from outsiders and forced religious conversion. Today, residents live in modern houses and work at many different jobs, but the community as a whole maintains a connection to their traditions, their ancestors, and the clay from Mother Earth.

NOTES FROM THE AUTHORS

I am the eldest great-grandchild of Maria and Julian Martinez. They were traditional Tewa people. I had the honor and privilege of living with my great-grandmother from age four to the fourth grade, and Maria's capacity for sharing her clay knowledge, and her experience as a traditional leader of women, had a profound impact on me. She stressed learning as a key aspect of life. The signature on my pottery is Tahnmoowhe, or Sunbeam, my Tewa name, given to me by my great-grandmother at birth. Six generations of Maria and Julian's descendants continue the legacy of black pottery today. The future is in their hands.

—Barbara Gonzales

I grew up hearing about the famous pottery of Maria Martinez from my grandmother, who was a member of the Osage Nation and collected Native American Indian art. After earning degrees in art and multicultural education, I became an art teacher and wanted to teach my students about Maria, but I had a hard time finding resources about her to use with children. While researching Maria, I found Barbara's name, and we connected over a desire to write a children's book about her great-grandmother. I'm thrilled to help bring the story of this amazing woman artist to life for a new generation.

—Anna Harber Freeman

SELECTED SOURCES

Krepela, Rick, dir. *Maria Martinez: Indian Pottery of San Ildefonso*. Cortez, CO: Interpark, 1972. VHS.

Maloof, Alfreda Ward. *Recollections from My Time in the Indian Service, 1935–1943: Maria Martinez Makes Pottery*. Klamath River, CA: Living Gold Press, 1997.

Marriott, Alice. *Maria: The Potter of San Ildefonso*. Norman, OK: University of Oklahoma Press, 1948.

Museum of New Mexico. 2002. "Touched by Fire: The Art, Life, and Legacy of Maria Martinez." http://www.indianartsandculture.org/exhibits/maria/.

Peterson, Susan. *The Living Tradition of Maria Martinez*. Tokyo: Kodansha International, 1978.

To my family: my supportive parents, my loving husband, and my incredible boys.

—AHF

To the memory of Maria Povika, my great-grandmother who will always have a place
in my artistic heart, and to all the people who love pottery.

Ku-daa—Thank you.

—Barbara "Tahnmoowhe" Gonzales

For my father, Bradford James Messer, who molded and shaped me.
I carry your memory in my heart.

—A

Library of Congress Cataloging-in-Publication data is on file with the publisher.

Text copyright © 2021 by Anna Harber Freeman and Barbara Gonzales
Illustrations copyright © 2021 by Aphelandra Messer
First published in the United States of America in 2021 by Albert Whitman & Company
ISBN 978-0-8075-7599-4 (hardcover) ✦ ISBN 978-0-8075-7601-4 (ebook)
Printed in China
10 9 8 7 6 5 4 WKT 26 25 24 23 22

Art and design by Aphelandra

For more information about Albert Whitman & Company,
visit our website at www.albertwhitman.com.